Calm
in
Chaos

Calm in *Chaos*

Prose on Tensions of Hate and Distrust in Society

Dr. Cheryl Green

WESTBOW
P R E S S®
A DIVISION OF THOMAS NELSON
& ZONDERVAN

WestBow Press books may be ordered through booksellers or by contacting:

WestBow Press
A Division of Thomas Nelson & Zondervan
1663 Liberty Drive
Bloomington, IN 47403
www.westbowpress.com
1 (866) 928-1240

ISBN: 978-1-9736-7080-3 (sc)
ISBN: 978-1-9736-7081-0 (e)

Library of Congress Control Number: 2019910713

Print information available on the last page.

WestBow Press rev. date: 8/19/2019

Calm in Chaos

Peer Reviews

The poems in "Calm in Chaos" are short in length, but are powerful nonetheless. Many of the poems evoke the pain of "otherness", of being subtly excluded, while also pointing to the various emperors who have no clothes. "Sadness" is felt viscerally. "Television" reflects the lack of transparency in our ever seemingly transparent world. These poems also evoke knowledge and belief in self in the face of adversity. They also reflect the yearning many of us have: reconciliation, polite debate, openness, and understanding. There's a lot of depth in this slim volume.

Donna Morelli, Esq., MSW, LICSW
Attorney
Licensed Clinical Social Worker

With this manuscript, Dr. Green has deliberately and with purpose elucidated the human experience of a person of color. Cheryl's appreciation of the world from this viewpoint brings to light a lingering stigma or bias that she dares to challenge with her brilliant mind while recognizing that some only view the color of skin. If you are looking for guidance to navigate this world as a person of color, you have found it.

Tanya Mary Smith, BSN, RN
Registered Nurse

I have just read through this manuscript, and I truly enjoyed it. The content is heartbreaking, uplifting, affirming, forgiving, forthcoming, and thought provoking.

When reading **Color,** the words used created a feeling of discrimination nurturing and yielding self-doubt. **Sadness** was the by-product of the reality of **Color** manifesting and producing vulnerability. As a woman of color, the poem **Courage** resonates with me. When faced with adversity there is no other option but to stand strong. One goes without, putting themselves last, going through untimely life changing events. But the world does not stop for anyone, so one does the best they can to carry on and stand strong.

Keeping in mind certain life experiences and re-reading **Courage**, one could see how **Health Disparities** is relative to the aforementioned. One goes to the doctor, reports any number of symptoms and is dismissed because of the biases and false perceptions erroneously incorporated into practice by the provider.

I loved **Mediocre** as it speaks to knowing one's worth. Many people will bask in the need to tell others what they should and should not or can and cannot do. The person that knows one's own worth can never falter. The placement for **Loud** after **Mediocre** was well done. As a professional it can be exhausting to work in an environment where you are one of few or the only one. Calm demeanor may get misinterpreted for having an attitude or lacking knowledge. Expressing something one is passionate about may be misconstrued as being loud. These misnomers can give way to **Isolation**.

After reading Biased **Faith** the thought came to mind, "if you don't stand for something you fall for anything". Biased Faith can lead to **Destruction**. Destruction read to me as the tale of the substance abuser lead by Biased Faith towards the path to destruction.

Thrive serves a reminder that for those with drive, failure is not an option. When reading **My Rock** there is salvation for the sadness, for the **Shadow People** who are the gifted ultimate survivors. **Weathered** reminds one that self-preservation is imperative to remaining calm, grounded giving way to **Resolution** or piece of mind.

Silence and **Plague** are prime examples of how respectful reciprocating communication is key to fixing any relationship, professional or personal.

The stories are succinct and to the point. For myself

re-reading was key to getting a better understanding. I really like the font and style of writing for the headings. Although some of the stories are direct in meaning, other stories will be left to the readers' interpretation. I also like the order in which the stories are placed. Starting in a place of uncertainty and angst with **Color**, and ending up with a solution in **Spaces**.

The book is a quick read and times when I was not clear on the intent of the prose, I re-read and was better able to understand. You are very talented Dr. Green.

Zubaida Dabre, MSN, RN, BA
Psychiatric Registered Nurse
Clinical Research Nurse

Foreword

For many reasons I am delighted and honored to write this foreword for the incomparable Dr. Cheryl Green. We met as young, enthusiastic undergraduates at Our Lady of the Elms College nearly 33 years ago, and even with career aspirations, marriages and rearing children, have managed to maintain a most cherished friendship.

I strongly believe in the uplifting and profound messages in "Calm in Chaos." Through Dr. Green's writings she manages to effectively touch on the many complex challenges faced day to day from "Color" to "Safety," and gives thought provoking meditations for managing and overcoming obstacles. This book is truly life transforming! It is written clearly and effortlessly flows from one commanding relevant topic to another. As a reader you are eager to move forward, but conflicted with the desire to re-read the passages and ponder the words. Nearly 11 years ago at 27 weeks gestation, I prematurely gave birth to my son who weighed a mere 2 pounds and spent the first 4 ½ months of his life in neonatal intensive care. It was during those dark and uncertain days that I could have undoubtedly found great comfort in Dr. Green's writings "Alive for a Reason" and "A Season."

I am however forever grateful for Dr. Green's prayers and encouraging words that spoke and continues to speak life into me and my son. Dr. Green is a living testament of her writings.

Enjoy this book and be blessed!
Trena Walton Bethune, MS
Director of Operations

Contents

Color

A calm.
Constant echoing in my brain.
Sinister plots against me. Paranoia rains.

Skin not like their own.
All that separates us.
Not the same.
Not as bright.
Not wanted.

Color.
Should not matter.
Yet, it does.

Sadness

A hollow entered into.
Specific pain unclear.
I seek my own interpretation.
Tears unplanned.
And sadness thick, all because I could not fit in.
Even if I tried.

Courage

Emboldened.
Spiny projections.
Posture strong.

A body and soul caving at times under
the weight of a heavy load.
Posture strong.

Disease, illness, and sadness.
Posture strong.

Raise my family.
Feed them too.
Posture strong.

I survive because I have courage.
Moreover, my posture is strong.

Heard You

I heard you when you said unkind words about me.
I in my own foolishness hid my face in shame.
Tears streamed.
I felt unworthy.

I heard you murmur my name behind a closed door.
You laughed with someone else.
Cannot hurt me but for a minute.

Memories of what I heard expire in a mind
focused on what is right, good, and true.

I heard you.
Nevertheless, I will be o.k.
The only thing wounded was my cars,
not what lies between them.

Mediocre

Mediocrity is the over simplicity of a life lived in absence
of self-acknowledgement of equality and quality.

Less is an option accepted when one
denigrates their own worth.
Subject to listening to that which is ignorant,
makes one vulnerable to the mediocre.

The ignorant are seldom silent as they seek to impose
their views of whom they determine to be mediocre.
However, the ignorant, like a slithering
serpent, will use whispers in an attempt to
condemn that which they are afraid.

Wise is the person who grapples with mediocrity
and holds it accountable. The ignorant will
then lose all self-imposed power.

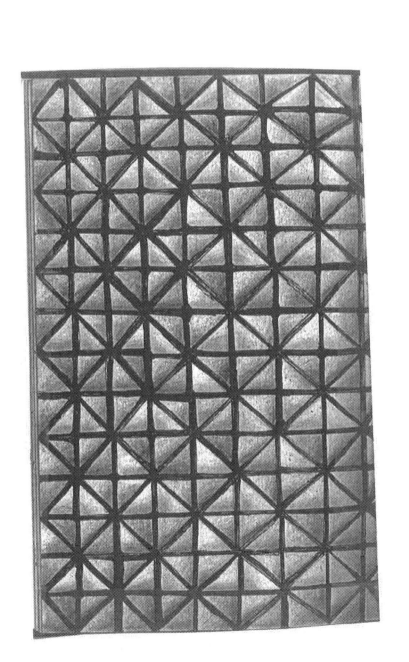

Loud

At a meeting and raised my hand today to ask a question.
Have not asked a question in four months.
Often sitting in silence.
A listening ear and notes taken.
I learn.

Calm down!
What question do you pose?

Shocked.
Voice never raised.
Mom and Dad taught me, never be rude.
Yet, labeled as loud.

Back in my office.
Dumbfounded.
A fellow worker approaches me.
Shakes his head in silence.
And shares, "That was a good idea."

Television

Hard to watch.
Visuals of hate, violence, and terror.

How does one ascribe ratings to that which
admonishes human pain, suffering, and hatred?
A society lost in its own visions and perceptions of reality.
Yet, we watch as others portray the
truth on a screen made of glass.

The irony being, the glass is absent of transparency.

Shadow People

You are precious.
A history unknown.
Skin of many colors.
Tongues speaking many languages.
You seek recognition for needs unmet.

In your silence and need, your brilliance is unknown.
Your gifts undiscovered.

A home is not yours at this time.
However, I understand, a home is not
always the answer for your pain.

A life lived before entering the shadows.
Bills paid and a job too.
No alcohol or drugs.
No weapons, no war, no relationships gone astray.
You are much more than the shadows in which you dwell.
You are priceless, though you have
nowhere to call your home.

Health Disparities

Went to the doctor.
Language and culture misunderstood.

In pain.
Asked by a nurse if I use opioids or drugs.
I only take vitamins.

Instructed to stop eating spicy foods and avoid frying.
I am a vegetarian.
I use turmeric and cumin to flavor my
foods and for medicinal purposes.

Told nothing is wrong with me.
Stressed, psychosomatic origins of the pain.

Three Months later.
The pain intensified.
Vomiting blood.
Cancer throughout my body.
Told, "I am sorry."

Health disparities.

Isolation

Compartmentalized because my ideas differ.
A smirk shared between co-workers as I offer my insights.

Isolated in my own intellect.
My opinion matters according to a quota.

No favors done for me if I symbolize workplace diversity.
Nevertheless, can contribute nothing according to those
who attempt to deem themselves greater than themselves.

Biased Faith

Man and womankind alike manufacture a religion.
Close-minded.

Where is God?

Not accepted, but faith tells me God accepts me for myself.
Will hate religion, maybe God too if I do not runaway.

Biased Faith seeks to entrap.
Stupefies the soul and the mind.
Embattles the body.

False religion.
Preached by a kind face mimicking Godly gestures.

Freedom can only come when the Real God
is asked by me to forgive my sins.
Cleanse my unrighteousness.
Teach me to forgive others.
Even those with Biased Faith.

Amen.

Destruction

Wars planned in the minds of those desiring destruction.
Human death.

Life not seen as a treasure.
Non-existence justified by false beliefs.

Emphasis on wants and desires.
No value for that which has a conscious,
and lives and breathes.

No answers in destruction.
Only the perpetuation of more destruction, more tears.

Dreams lost and nothing gained.

Old Age

No honor given to that, which ages.
Beauty goes in reverse.

A surgeon's knife hosts the change in time.
Skin pealed, poked, plumped and sutured.

Wisdom forsaken.
The new deemed as innovative, yet
we live history in reverse.
We repeat the past.

Afraid to age, to have lived.
What was honor in the color grey is now hidden
amidst dyes, creams, injections, and surgeries.
Hiding what I inevitably will become.
Old.

Different Love

Fell in love.
Two different worlds.

Cannot imagine a world without you.
Told that your very existence will hurt me.
My future, my life will not amount to much.
Skin too dark.
Skin too light.

Brain not smart enough.
Slough is believed to inhabit that which is different.
Ignorance too.

Not sure anymore would care when I reflect on our society,
Whether I should love you.
Two different people.

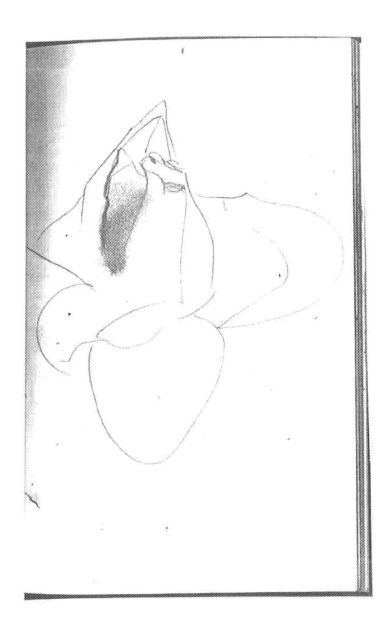

Kindred

In-kind.
More alike than not.
Disconnects unite us in a union aligned.
Kindred, yet differences bring us together.

Alive for A Reason

Survived the tides that swelled and tumbled upon me.
Flood waters that seemed never to diminish or subside.
Not alone.
God promised to stay with me.
Walked through the waters filled with resistance.
I persevered.
The waters are now subsiding. I walk upright. No waters
    near nor above my head.
I have survived.

A Season

This is only a season.

The pain of this present experience will past.

A light of hope will emerge.

The wound in her my heart will heal.

The sorrow in my gut will cry no more.

I will soon recall my pain in a story of reflection.

I expect to weather this season.

I have experienced seasons before and know the power of
unwavering faith.

You see, this season will be no more and I will be a victor.

Blessed

Cannot tell you what I been through.
Not easy being labelled different.
Persecuted not because of what you know, but what
    another perceives that you should not know.

Cannot be angry.
Tears stream in silence.
Tired.

I know that I am blessed.
God told me so.
So, I can survive this mess.
Did you hear me, God said I was blessed!

Confused

Confused by the hatred.
No hatred shared between us.
It appears the hatred comes solely from you.

I am not obliged to treat you the same.
My soul will not allow me to hate you.
My mind renewed has willed it not to.

You are confused.
You think you have power over all.
Narcissism blinds you and makes you confused.

Righteous

Clean.
God told me despite my faults, he forgives me.

Righteous, not certain I qualify.
Broken.

Ready.
Ready to be forgiven.
Not sure I am deserving.

Learning.
Despite my inadequacies, God loves me.
I am perfect.

Received

Rejected by a society that classifies me as worthless,
  suspicious, and void of opinion.
Belief in humanity and its goodness I receive.

Cursed by others for the texture of my hair, the color of my
  skin, and the language I speak.
Gracious hope in the handshake or smile of a stranger, I
  receive.

Judged by others as incompetent and unable to do my job.
Rewarded for my hard work and integrity.

I receive the good.
Because I am determined to not be deterred by that which
  I should not receive.
I know who I am.

Respecter of Persons

Respect.
Not a burden.
A human being deserves and is worthy of living.

Respect.
A heart beats.
Movement in closed spaces.
A human being worthy of life worth living.

Conception.
Chaos in the womb.
A human being is worth living.

Principals

Standing for what I believe in.
Listening to what you believe in as well.

Respect.
Anger avoided as we share words.
Minds process that which has meaning initially to the
     deliverer.
The receiver listens.

Judgement not needed.
Judgement not necessary.
Judgement without power.

In silence I listen to what you say.
I do so without judgement because I respect you.

Right or wrong?
I guess this means we both have judgement.
Perhaps it is necessary to determine our own morality.

Or perhaps our morality is only determined by God.

Thrive

We are all on earth to thrive.
Our potential is unlimited.
Hindered by finite minds that attempt to undermine our
existence.

Hindered by our own insecurities.
We can thrive.
It is merely a decision to defeat that which has no right to
define who we are.
Our right to exist.

Strongholds.
Can be both physical, mental, and emotional.

Death Not in Me

Death is not in me.
It left my soul a long time ago.

Surrounded by violence.
In my neighborhood.
My home.
My workplace.

Death seeks to enter within.
Not wanted, death lingers.
Waiting.

Death has no dominion over me and must flee.

Survived

Overcome by what is the journey of today.
Survive I must, to see another day.
Hidden beneath a heart of sorrow.
Frightened by the prospects of what I must complete.
I recall past successes.

A harvest awaits me if I complete the journey.
If I learn from the complexities of life.
I survive.

Loved

Expecting love from others.
Depleted of self-love from the critics.
You are loved.

Measured by perceived accomplishments.
How is success truly measured?
Is it consequential?

Conditional acceptance and love is frivolous.
What deems one complete, whole?
Loved.

My Rock

Sustainer.
Visible to me.

Real.
Protector of my soul.
Shield for my weaknesses.
Promise for my hopelessness.

I seek you.
My Rock.
My fortress.

Rebellion

A spirit whose purpose is to bring discord.
Kind regard to few.
Or no one.

Respect unknown.
Blind foresight.
Neutrality in absence of favor.

The reveler has few allies.
Takes many prisoners.
Believes integrity to not be an option.

Rebellion defeats itself.
In a solemn act of isolation, it disappears.
Remembered no more and without legacy.

Silence

Bewilderment of echoes.
Sound waves without exit.
He sits quietly as if without existence.

Buffered by soundproof minds.
She considers her words.

The problem with silence is that it bleeds ignorance.
Silence.

Weathered

Uncontrolled storms, blizzards, and floods.
Fatigued beyond the understanding of rest.

Worn by the changes of the inclement.
Beaten by hailstones of angry words.

I am weathered.
I seek a way to end the cycle.
Realizing that weather will change.
I must protect myself from the elements.

Plague

Hatred is a plague that left untreated, can grow to
   pandemic proportions.
Riots.
Violence.
Blanket stares of anger, distress.
Social distance.
Spiritual lies.
Maltreatment.

I avoid you.
You avoid me.
Unity avoided.
Not meant to be.
And determined, only by me.

Resolution

Brightness.
Light.
Cannot deny the truth.

Resolved to confront that which I thought I hate.
I place that which intimidates me under a microscope.
Increasing the resolution.
A wavelength of light.

I hated without logic, reason, or analysis.
Cannot profess mental brilliance when I hate.

Hate itself perpetuates the societal belief of greater than.
Greater than whom or what?

Resolution brings clarity.
It exposes the ugly in the human soul.

Resolve to live in resolution.

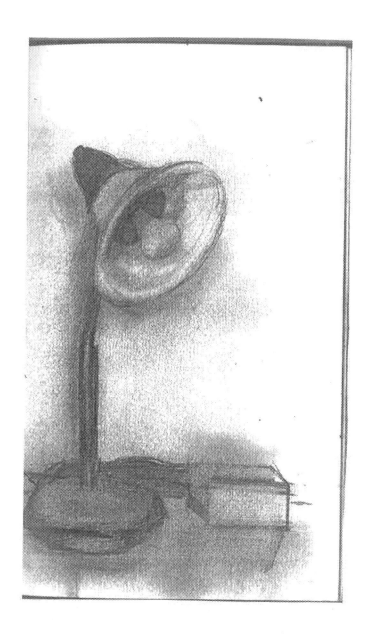

Encouraged

Acceptance that I am not the same as you are.
That I am o.k.
That you are o.k.

Encouraged that healing can occur.
Open discussions.
Honest thoughts expressed.

Reaching out to you.
Despite your self-imposed walls.
Hoping to help you climb over our barriers.

Encouraged that we can seek peace.

Spaces

Neighborhoods segregated.
Poverty too.
Options are open.
Doors closed based upon false perceptions.

Spaces.
Not defined.
Spaces contain people with limitless abilities.

We must agree to enter one another's spaces.
Entering spaces causes vulnerability.
Eliminates division.
Destroys prejudices.

Let's agree to enter one another's spaces.
Let's unite in a union of friendship and trust.

Printed in the United States
By Bookmasters